Greater Than a Tourist Book Series Reviews from Readers

I think the series is wonderful and beneficial for tourists to get information before visiting the city.

-Seckin Zumbul, Izmir Turkey

I am a world traveler who has read many trip guides but this one really made a difference for me. I would call it a heartfelt creation of a local guide expert instead of just a guide.

-Susy, Isla Holbox, Mexico

New to the area like me, this is a must have!

-Joe, Bloomington, USA

This is a good series that gets down to it when looking for things to do at your destination without having to read a novel for just a few ideas.

-Rachel, Monterey, USA

Good information to have to plan my trip to this destination.

-Pennie Farrell, Mexico

Aptly titled, you won't just be a tourist after reading this book. You'll be greater than a tourist!

-Alan Warner, Grand Rapids, USA

Thank you for a fantastic book.

-Don, Philadelphia, USA

SMITHER

Great ideas for a port day.
-Mary Martin USA

Even though I only have three days to spend in San Miguel in an upcoming visit, I will use the author's suggestions to guide some of my time there. An easy read - with chapters named to guide me in directions I want to go.
-Robert Catapano, USA

Great insights from a local perspective! Useful information and a very good value!
-Sarah, USA

This series provides an in-depth experience through the eyes of a local. Reading these series will help you to travel the city in with confidence and it'll make your journey a unique one.
-Andrew Teoh, Ipoh, Malaysia

Tourists can get an amazing "insider scoop" about a lot of places from all over the world. While reading, you can feel how much love the writer put in it.
-Vanja Živković, Sremski Karlovci, Serbia

GREATER THAN A TOURIST – WUHAN HUBEI CHINA

50 Travel Tips from a Local

John Smither

SMITHER

Cover designed by

Greater Than a Tourist
Visit our website at www.GreaterThanaTourist.com

Lock Haven, PA

ISBN: 9781977074799

>TOURIST

50 TRAVEL TIPS FROM A LOCAL

SMITHER

BOOK DESCRIPTION

Are you excited about planning your next trip?
Do you want to try something new?
Would you like some guidance from a local?

If you answered yes to any of these questions, then this Greater Than a Tourist book is for you.

Greater Than a Tourist- Wuhan Hubei China by John Smither offers the inside scoop on Wuhan. Most travel books tell you how to travel like a tourist. Although there is nothing wrong with that, as part of the Greater Than a Tourist series, this book will give you travel tips from someone who has lived at your next travel destination.

In these pages, you will discover advice that will help you throughout your stay. This book will not tell you exact addresses or store hours but instead will give you excitement and knowledge from a local that you may not find in other smaller print travel books.

Travel like a local. Slow down, stay in one place, and get to know the people and the culture. By the time you finish this book, you will be eager and prepared to travel to your next destination.

SMITHER

TABLE OF CONTENTS

DEDICATION

This book is dedicated to the people of Wuhan for welcoming me into their lives, making the city feel like home and treating me like a local.

SMITHER

ABOUT THE AUTHOR

John Smither is a freelance writer and teacher from the UK who now lives most of the year in Wuhan his adopted home. He has lived there since 2014 and when he is not teaching he uses it as a base to explore the region and further afield taking in his loves of travel and history. Ha also has a home in the city of Yingtan in nearby Jiangxi province which he shares with his wife and son. It is unusual for a foreigner to live so long in one place in China, so for this reason he is treated like a local by his many friends in the city.

SMITHER

HOW TO USE THIS BOOK

The Greater Than a Tourist book series was written by someone who has lived in an area for over three months. The goal of this book is to help travelers either dream or experience different locations by providing opinions from a local. The author has made suggestions based on their own experiences. Please do your own research before traveling to the area in case the suggested places are unavailable.

SMITHER

FROM THE PUBLISHER

Traveling can be one of the most important parts of a person's life. The anticipation and memories that you have are some of the best. As a publisher of the Greater Than a Tourist book series, as well as the popular 50 Things to Know book series, we strive to help you learn about new places, spark your imagination, and inspire you. Wherever you are and whatever you do I wish you safe, fun, and inspiring travel.

Lisa Rusczyk Ed. D.
CZYK Publishing

SMITHER

OUR STORY

Traveling is a passion of the "Greater than a Tourist" series creator. Lisa studied abroad in college, and for their honeymoon Lisa and her husband toured Europe. During her travels to Malta, an older man tried to give her some advice based on his own experience living on the island since he was a young boy. She was not sure if she should talk to the stranger but was interested in his advice. When traveling to some places she was wary to talk to locals because she was afraid that they weren't being genuine. Through her travels, Lisa learned how much locals had to share with tourists. Lisa created the "Greater Than a Tourist" book series to help connect people with locals. A topic that locals are very passionate about sharing.

SMITHER

WELCOME TO
> TOURIST

SMITHER

INTRODUCTION

"The world is a book, and those who do not travel read only one page." – Saint Augustine

I feel very lucky to have led the life I have had, to travel the world and see so many places, my travel experiences have been mostly through working abroad and then relishing each new place and learning all I can about that location whilst I am there.

I particularly like the experience of cycle touring, traveling slowly and discovering things that are easily missed when using motorized transport or flying directly to the next destination. For me, going to work in Wuhan was a sudden change of plan as I had been expecting to work elsewhere, I hope through this book I can give you an insight into why I enjoy living in Wuhan and that it inspires you to come and visit the city.

SMITHER

1. When Is The Best Time To Visit Wuhan

The summer months in Wuhan are hot and oppressive, the city is also known as one of four furnace cities in China. Summer temperatures can often reach 40C with hot and humid days and regular heavy rain showers. The springtime from March until May is one of color when flowers are in blossom and with comfortable temperatures it is a pleasant time to walk in the many parks in the city. The autumn (fall) months of September through to November are also a popular time for visitors after the heat of the summer.

2. Ask a Local Where Are The Best Places To Stay

Wuhan is a very large city with literally thousands of options of where to stay, from budget hotels and hostels up to the most luxurious penthouse suites. Two of the best areas to stay are close to Zhongshan Park (on the Metro line 2) with good choices of hotels, good shopping opportunities and a place to relax in the park. The second option of where to stay is the area around the Han Street Walking Plaza and New Wanda Shopping Mall. The area is close to Chuhe Hanjie Station on Metro line 4. If a lively night life is important to you then you will enjoy the choices of night clubs, cafes and bars. A store in the basement of the Wanda Mall has a large variety of imported goods that are difficult to find in China.

3. One Of China's Top Locations To Study

Wuhan is a great city for students with over one million students from across the world studying at the 80 universities in the city. There are students from more than 100 countries that come to Wuhan to continue their studies at university. The high number of international students helps to contribute to Wuhan being an international city.

4. Understanding The Yangtze River

During a visit to Wuhan you should not miss taking a leisurely boat trip along the Yangtze River. You will be able to witness how busy the river is to commercial river traffic with large industrial barges plying their trade up and down one of the world's most famous rivers. Observe the riverfront buildings built to European styles dating from the 1930's when the city's waterfront was under foreign concessions to increase overseas trade.

5. Hot Dry Noodles

Every province in China will make the claim that their food is the best in China. Wuhan's culinary favorite is Hot Dry Noodles or rè gān miàn. Hot Dry Noodles are a breakfast food in Wuhan but can be eaten all day as a satisfying snack. The freshly cooked noodles are mixed with oil and then dried. To reheat they are placed into boiling water then removed from the water and mixed with soy sauce, sesame paste, chopped garlic, chives and chili oil. Many vendors will make their own signature taste to the noodles they produce to make their product a little different from that of their competitors.

6. Wuhan Style Duck Neck

Wuhan's style of the popular dish, Duck's Neck or Ya Bozi is popular throughout China. It is often called spicy duck neck due to the extremely spicy flavor giving it a unique color of deep reddish brown. Many tourists when departing the city to travel home will take this dish with them. Whenever I visit some Chinese friends in Guangdong province I have to take a plentiful supply of this dish with me for them to quickly consume upon my arrival.

7. Should I Take An Umbrella Today

Even on the sunniest days you should carry an umbrella with you, the weather can change so quickly in Wuhan and showers of rain can occur when they are least expected. The hot summer months are when the heaviest rainfall occurs and temporary localized flooding can block your way. When it is not raining you may want to carry your umbrella to protect yourself from the sun.

8. The 3 Gorges Dam

A visit to Wuhan would not be complete without taking an excursion to the world famous Three Gorges Dam. From Wuhan you will need to take a fast train to Yichang city. There are up to 80 trains each day and the fast train takes just 2 hours. When exiting the train you will need to take a bus to Sandouping and the Dam itself. The 3 Gorges Dam is the world's largest hydropower project, with firsts in being efficient in flood control of the lower stages of the river and the world's biggest migration project when thousands of people had to move to new homes due to the new lake forming behind the dam. The dam is 607 feet tall, and 3,319 yards wide at the top. It was built in three stages taking 17 years to be completed after construction began in 1992.

9. Wuhan's First Yangtze River Bridge

Wuhan currently has seven bridges and two tunnels across the Yangtze River. The 'First Bridge' was built in 1957; it is a double tiered bridge with a double rail line running below a four lane road. This was the first bridge across the Yangtze River not just in Wuhan but across the mighty river, its construction reduced journey times by several hours. Trains to and from the north stopped at Hankou station, those to the south began at Wuchang. The bridge eased the congestion on the river of people and goods being ferried across. The bridge is 5,511 feet or 1,680 meters in length. The two tunnels are both used by Wuhan Metro and line 2 was the first metro line to be submerged below the river.

10. Yellow Crane Tower

The Yellow Crane Tower is one of the symbols of Wuhan and its number one tourist attraction. The first tower was built in 223AD, with the current building being completed in 1985 on Snake Hill in Wuchang, about 1km away from the site of the original tower. Two versions exist as to the origins of the name, one that it was built at Yellow Crane Jetty, alongside the river. The second legend that Wang Zi'an, an immortal, rode away from the tower on a yellow crane and stopped on his way at Snake Hill.

The tower has been destroyed and rebuilt at least 12 times due to fire and warfare. It was repaired ten times during the dynasties of Ming and Qing. The last tower at the original site was destroyed in 1884. A new tower was reconstructed from 1981, and completed 101 years after the previous one was destroyed.

The top level of the tower has views across the nearby river and surrounding areas; the tower looks like an ancient monument but is modern in design including an elevator for elderly of infirm visitors.

11. Do Not Rush

Do not rush about, relax and take your time. Most Chinese people tend to walk a little slower than westerners; this is often due to the heat. The best advice is to go with the flow and walk at the speed of others. It is often very crowded particularly in the city center, take your time and take in the sights of the city.

12. Take A Trip On Wuhan Metro

Wuhan Metro is very clean and modern with 7 lines currently in operation; there are plans for this to be increased to 25 lines making it one of the world's largest metro systems. The roads of Wuhan can be extremely busy, particularly in the busiest periods of the morning and early evening, the metro is a good fast and efficient option particularly if you need to cross the Yangtze River. The metro can become extremely busy at peak travel times. There is a rule on Wuhan's metro of no food or drink to be consumed, this helps to keep the trains and platform areas clean and free of the strong odours of some Chinese food. The easiest way for visitors to travel on the metro is to buy tickets as they are needed, tickets must be retained and deposited into the exit gate to exit the station when you complete your journey. Ticket machines are in English and the metro is probably the easiest way to navigate your way around the city if you do not speak Chinese.

13. Using Local Buses

Traveling by bus in Wuhan can be quite an experience and not for all. The buses can get extremely busy and you will not get the personal space you would like or are used to. They are however, cheap and regular. On most routes you will not wait longer than 10 minutes for a bus, and do not be surprised if 2 or even 3 arrive almost together. There is no English used on the bus so you will need to know the bus number of the service you require. A good tip is to count the number of stops until your exit or have the destination stop written in Chinese for you and show this to someone on the bus, most people will be very happy to help you.

14. Cycling Around Wuhan

If you are staying in Wuhan for more than a few days you might want to upload an app onto your phone that allows you to use one of the thousands of dock less bikes that are available across the city. If you require a bike but cannot see one, then the use of GPS will show you the location of the nearest bike available. They are a cheap option for getting around the city you should just remember to lock the wheel mechanism when you have finished or you will continue to be charged. There are several companies operating this service in Wuhan and some of them give an initial month free of charge, ideal if you are only visiting for a short period of time.

15. Three Cities In One

Wuhan is actually an amalgamation of three cities divided by the Yangtze and Han Rivers. Wuchang is to the east of the Yangtze, Hanyang and Hankou are to the west of the river and divided by the Han River as it merges with the larger river at this point. They were each referred to as a separate city until 1927 when the name Wuhan was derived from the first syllable of each city, chosen by the National Government during Wuhan's short term as the capital of China.

16. Three Main Railway Stations In Wuhan

There are three major railway stations in Wuhan, the newest station is Wuhan in the north east of the city in Hongshan district. Wuchang railway station is more central and on the same side of the river while Hankou railway station is across the river and to the north of the city. Each railway station is several kilometers apart and care should be taken to ensure you go to the correct station.

Wuchang and Wuhan stations are both on line 4 of the city's metro system and you should allow at least 40 minutes when traveling from one to another. Hankou railway station is on line 2 and can be reached from the other two stations by changing lines at Zhongnan Road or Hongshan Square stations. To reach Hankou from Wucheng you should allow an hour journey time, with just over an hour needed to go from Hankou to Wuhan.

17. Be Friendly and Smile

By learning a few simple phrases in Chinese, such as hello (ni hao), goodbye (zai jian) or thank you (xie xie) your stay in China can be much more rewarding. Smile when people greet you and they will then be more open, friendly and smile back. Many Chinese people are curious as to why you are visiting their country and want to practice their English with you. Most people do not know any English other than a few basic greetings or what is your name, how old are you or where are you from?

It can be tiring hearing the same questions over and over again, this is where a friendly smile comes in and if you know a little Chinese most people are impressed by that.

18. Shopping

I am not particularly a fan of shopping and will go out and buy what I need when I need it and get whatever shopping I need as quickly as possible. In Wuhan there are several large shopping malls and shopping areas. Most of the leading fashion and designers brands are available although some will not be genuine, counterfeit goods are prevalent throughout China and Wuhan is no exception to that. If you come to Wuhan and shop for clothes or other goods you may well find a bargain but the authenticity of that bargain may well come into question.

19. Bartering At The Market

Every district within Wuhan has a market where you can practice bartering for your goods, if you think the price you have been quoted is too high counter it with a lower bid. You may get a lower price. If you are not happy with the price, or you feel you are being overcharged simply walk away and try it again at another stall. Often by walking away (if you are being overcharged) the stallholder will immediately drop their asking price to avoid missing out on a sale. Stores such as supermarkets that have prices displayed will generally not accept bartering. Clothing stores, anywhere that sells electrical goods or souvenirs are usually good for bartering.

20. Street Food

The street food in Wuhan is in my opinion well worth the experience; these are usually mobile stalls that set up in the evening and continue until late or the early morning in some cases. Some stalls will sell you the food and you then walk as you eat, others will set up tables and chairs and you can sit, chat and relax over a beer or two. The Shao Kao or Chinese Barbeque is usually various meat products on skewers, vegetables and fish. It is usually spicy, although you can ask for non-spicy food if you prefer. With a group of friends this is a great way to pass a few hours during the evening.

21. Play Or Watch Mahjong

The game of Mahjong is played extensively across China and in Wuhan you do not need to walk too far before you will come across a group of people and in the center of that group will be four people playing mahjong. In addition to outdoor games there are some indoor rooms set up for the exclusive use of playing mahjong. The game is played with 144 tiles, between 4 players and each player begins with 13 tiles. The idea of the game is to pick up a fresh tile, discard whichever one you do not want and to win you must have 3 groups of 4 tiles and a pair using the tile that is picked up. It is played very quickly, can be very noisy with tiles being discarded and each round of the game is played for a wager or stake. I like to watch this game being played, but the pace of the game is much too fast for me to participate.

22. Tea Houses

There are several tea houses in Wuhan, some are within shopping malls and their primary use is to invite you to drink tea with the intention that you will buy at least one pack of tea. If you do not buy any tea you will have to pay for the tea you have consumed. My favorite type of tea houses are where you sit down, pay a set price and drink tea for one or two hours with the tea pot being continually topped up or refreshed. One of the best places to take in this relaxing pursuit is close to the river, sitting outside on a warm afternoon.

23. Happy Valley

Wuhan's Happy Valley theme park is located in Hongshan district and is close to Wuhan Railway Station. Wuhan Happy Valley opened in April 2012 and is the fifth location in China of this chain of theme parks. There are five roller coasters in the park, lots of other rides suitable for smaller children and 3D and 4D cinemas. If you buy the day pass everything is included in the price and you can go on each ride as many times as you like. It does get very crowded during Chinese holidays.

24. East Lake

The East Lake in Wuhan's Huazhong district is China's largest city lake covering an area of 88 square kilometers and receives around one million visitors each year. In addition to the lake itself there are several attractions in the vicinity of the lake, these include, Liyuan Park- a large area to the west of the lake with a free swimming area. There are two museums- the Hubei Provincial Museum and the Hubei Art Museum, as well as several parks and gardens. There are several causeways that cross the eastern part of the East Lake they provide fishing areas for locals with carp being the most popular catch. The lake is six times the size of the more famous West Lake in Hangzhou and is also a popular location for walking, cycling and jogging particularly among students from the two universities (Wuhan University and China University of Geosciences) that are adjacent to the lake.

Beneath the lake is a 6 lane road tunnel (Donghu Lake Tunnel), it is China's longest tunnel underneath a lake at 10.6 kilometers in length and takes a car around 15 minutes to drive through the tunnel.

25. Time To Visit A Temple

In Hanyang district you can visit Guiyuan Buddhist Temple on Cuiwei Road and close to Zhongjiachun metro stop on line 6. Leave the metro station from exit C, walk to the first intersection, turn right and the temple is a short distance along the road. The temple dates from the 17th century although there are many newer additions. There are a lot of steps to navigate and it can get very busy at weekends and on holidays, the best time to visit is during the week. Next to the entrance is a tourist information center where you can get maps of the temple and its grounds or even hire a guide.

26. Baotong Temple in Wuchang

Baotong Temple is another Buddhist temple in Wuhan and is accessible from Wuhan metro line 2 at Baotong Temple Station. The attractively laid out place of worship is particularly busy on Sundays when visiting monks from other local temples will congregate at Baotong for ritual chanting and prayers. Week days are less congested if you prefer the solitude of silence while you climb the 7 storied pagoda of Hongshan Tower with over 1000 years of history. Baotong Temple is less of a museum than some monasteries and more of a working temple. This temple is a great place to spend a few hours relaxing in tranquility while surrounded by the busy life of a fast paced city.

27. Visit Hubu Alley

Hubu Alley can be found on Ziyou Road in Wuchang district very close to the Yellow Crane Tower and the First Yangtze River Bridge, it is one of Wuhan's many food streets. There are over 200 food stalls selling a wide variety of foods, very cheaply. If you do not speak or read Chinese you are advised to go here with a Chinese speaking guide as several foods will be a mystery as to what they are or what they may contain. Even if you do not buy any of the snacks available, it is a great place to take a stroll and observe this daily ritual of many of Wuhan's residents. Some of the less palatable snacks may include intestines, duck or chicken heads and feet and countless varieties of tofu, some of the smells can be a little overpowering.

It is a great place to savor the atmosphere of local life in the morning or evening and after eating take a walk along the river nearby.

28. One Of Wuhan's Best Kept Secrets

The Han Show Theatre is a truly spectacular show; the theatre was specifically built to house the show that combines a solid stage and aquatic displays. It is located in Wuchang district on Chuhehan Street and is a short walk from Chu He Han Jie Station on metro line 4 and combines an acrobatic stage show with an aquatic show with divers and giant LED screens to give visual effects. The theatre has 2000 seats and the seats move during the performance to add to the effect of the audience appearing to participate in the show. The stage changes from an aquatic one into a dry stage or back again in just 80 seconds using hydraulic lifts. The story without giving too much away is of Ye Ming as he follows a quest to find the woman he loves, Jiaje. It is a story of loneliness, grief and happiness. Highly recommended but a little expensive for the majority of Wuhan people, it is also recommended to sit a little way back from the stage to see everything better.

29. Eat At Restaurants Recommended By Locals

Restaurants such as Kang LongTaiZi Jiu Xuan (JinRong) found at JianShe Avenue 711, Wuhan, China is part of a well established restaurant group in Wuhan that is very popular with locals and visitors.

The extensive menu is easy to follow as every dish has a picture and is accompanied by an English description of the ingredients. It has extremely cheap prices and is excellent quality. It serves lunches and dinner and can become very noisy when attended by large groups, if you want some privacy while eating then use one of the small rooms available.

30. Jianghan Road Walking Street

This popular walking street can be found in Wuhan's Jianghan district, just to the north of the Yangtze River, it is popular among locals and tourists. The walking street stretches about 500 meters from Xunlimen (lines 1 and 2) metro station to Jianghan Road (lines 2 and 6) metro station. The area around Jianghan Road metro station (along many of the small side roads) has some interesting colonial buildings built almost a century ago. The walking street is full of designer brands, many at much cheaper prices than found in western countries. Often during the evening there is the added bonus of street entertainers performing a variety of acts of varying quality, you should tip them only if you feel the performance deserves it. There are several cheap food stalls to be found in the surrounding streets and in the basement of the giant sized Wangfujing shopping mall. Although it is a walking street you should be cautious of the electrically powered e-bikes that are often driven along pedestrian walking areas.

31. Museums in Wuhan

Wuhan Museum is located on Qingnian Road in Hankou and just a few minute's walk away from Hankou Bus and Railway stations, it is open daily from 9am until 4pm and admission is free. To enter the museum your bags will be screened through x-ray machines and you must show your passport or other suitable ID at the security check. The museum is full of archaeological artifacts significant in the history of Wuhan and Hubei province. Audio guides are available in many languages although there are descriptions on several exhibits with some information in English.

Hubei Provincial Museum on Donghu Road, Wuchang is close to the East Lake and contains more than 140,000 items. These artifacts were excavated from a large tomb discovered nearby and are over 2400 years old. The museum explains the local history in a very detailed way, highly recommended and well worth a visit.

32. Beach Park

Wuhan is a long way from the sea and the beach park is a strip of sand alongside the Yangtze River close to Jianghan Road metro station on lines 2 and 6. It is a good place to relax during the late afternoon or early evening and people watch. After the sun has set the lights of the buildings across the river make for a spectacular setting, watch kite flying, or purchase your own and join in. Watch the Chinese ritual of dancing or groups practicing Tai Chi or use some of the free exercise equipment, all very good free entertainment as you spend a relaxing few hours away from the hustle and bustle of the city.

33. Mo Hill

Mo Hill is to the south east of East Lake and can be reached by bus numbers 3, 36, 59, 515 or 557, it covers an area of 5 square kilometers and is home to an abundance of plants and unique gardens as well as being a relic to the State of Chu, one of the earliest feudal dynasties in China from 221-206BC.

Historical reminders of the State of Chu include the city wall, market, gardens and crafts. The Botanical Garden holds 360 different types of plants in 13 different gardens including the Japanese Cherry Blossom garden. March, April and May are the best times of year to visit to see the Cherry Blossom at its best.

You can walk or take a small shuttle bus for a small fee to visit each area; there is also a small theme park with a few rides. It is an excellent spot to go and have a picnic while taking in the views of the city.

34. 1911 Wuchang Uprising

The Memorial Hall to the Wuchang Uprising that occurred in 1911 is an important monument to one of the keys moments in Chinese history. It is located to the south of the Yellow Crane Tower in Wuchang district. The uprising in1911 led to the fall of the ruling Qing dynasty and that led to the creation of modern China. The Revolutionary Army under the leadership of Sun Yat-Sen began their quest here that led to Sun Yat-Sen becoming the President of the Republic of China. His statue is in the plaza at the front of the Red Chamber, the main building housing the exhibits on display. There is free entry but you do need to show your passport, it is open daily from 9am until 5pm. There is a lot of information on the uprising with most of it available in English.

35. A Nice Park To Relax In

Hankou's Zhongshan Park is on Jiefang Road in Qiaokou district, it is a large green park in the middle of the busy city. A great place where there are quiet areas that you can just sit and relax while watching the people of Wuhan do their daily exercises or dancing. The center of the park has a large boating area on the lake. There is an amusement park with a small rollercoaster and several other rides mostly suitable for children. The Metro line 2 has a stop next to the entrance, the stop is named after the park and it is free entry.

36. International Shopping Plazas

The Spanish, German and Italian shopping plazas are part of a huge shopping area close to the Optic Valley Metro stop on line 2. It is currently the terminal station for that line and is very busy and will continue to be until the extension to line 2 is completed in 2019. The shopping plazas are full of expensive designer stores, but go up to the 2nd or 3rd floor dining areas and you will find some good restaurants. It is located at Guanggu BuXingJie in Wuchang's Optic Valley. There is a French plaza expected to be open by 2019.

37. Buskers And Beggars

Jiqing Street in Hankou's Jiang'an district is a mix of shops and restaurants, it is a great place to walk and observe the evening activity of dapaidang style dining (dining outdoors) while street musicians go from table to table hoping the diners will be enticed into listening to their music or song. The music ranges from classical Chinese to the latest Asian or western music.

They may be individual performers or small groups; they will be playing a variety of instruments and a varying quality. The best time to visit is during the spring or autumn (fall) when the weather is at its most favorable. Beware that in addition to those entertaining you for a small fee there are a group of beggars in attendance and they will home in on foreigners assuming they are rich, they will leave you alone eventually.

38. Misleading Information

There is some misleading information about the next attraction, Changchun Taoist Temple. You might think it should be in the city of Changchun, further to the north in Jilin province. It is located on the southern side of Shuangfeng Mountain, in Wuchang, there are no mountains in Wuchang, but it sounds more impressive than very small hill.

Changchun means longevity of spring and is written differently than the city of the same name in Chinese. It is unusual for a temple in China as it has lots of information written in English, the shrines are on different levels as the hill rises and at night it makes a pretty sight illuminated in the dark, surrounded by tall buildings.

39. The Largest Shopping Area In Wuhan

The city of Wuhan has several large shopping areas; the biggest has to be at GuangGu Square or Optic Valley as it is known by most foreigners in the city. The Valley Mall is a large part of that complex of malls that includes World City Plaza and International Plaza.

If you like crowded streets, full of bustling people than you will be at home here among the busy shopping centers, walking streets, designer brand stores and an endless choice of restaurants. A little difficult to find but deep inside this mall is the entrance to a large Carrefour supermarket on the 2nd and 3rd floors. There is also a multi screen cinema and a large selection of phone and computer outlets.

40. A Park Of Singing Birds

Jiefang Park located on Gongyuan Road, Jiang'an district in Wuhan is possibly the best park to be found in Wuhan. It has such a peaceful, calm and pleasant atmosphere particularly if you go during the week when the only people you are likely to see are elderly men who bring their caged birds with them. The cages are positioned hanging from tree branches and the pet birds will then sing to each other. The surrounding area is also one of beauty and helps to add to the park's attractive atmosphere of peace and tranquility.

41. The Coldest Place In Wuhan

Without doubt during the summer in Wuhan you want to find somewhere cool so you do not overheat in the furnace city. A good place to keep very cool is the Ice Museum inside the zoo. Wuhan's zoo may not be for everyone, although it has recently received some much needed maintenance work and conditions are now better than they were.

You should try to spend the whole day there; it is spread out over a large area although you can pay to use an electric cart to take you to the far side of the zoo to save on some walking. Inside there is a giant panda, really just the one! There are also some very large Siberian tigers, giraffes and kangaroos. The kangaroos share a paddock with some peacocks, and there is sometimes a standoff between the male peacocks as they strut about and the larger kangaroos. As your visit comes to an end it is somewhat refreshing to don an arctic coat and step into the Ice Museum, it is a pleasant way to complete your tour of the zoo.

42.Zhongshan Warship Museum

During the Battle of Wuhan in October 1938, Wuhan was under attack from Japanese forces. The gunboat Zhongshan was attacked by six aircraft, it shot down two before it sunk into the Yangtze River with 25 of the crew still onboard. In 1997 it was raised from the seabed and taken to a local shipyard to be restored. It now sits on display at a purpose built museum in Jiangxia district to the south of Wuchang.

The easiest way to reach the museum is by taxi, but it is quite a distance and the journey will not be less than 100RMB. You could take the bus, 910 from Wuchang Railway station will take you there for 3 RMB each. It is however 43 bus stops away and about 75 minutes, so I advise you to make sure you get a seat. I can assure you the long bus ride is worth it, you are able to see the warship from several levels and galleries exhibit several smaller items recovered from the seabed during the recovery process. The museum is surrounded by a well laid out lake and park with a memorial on a nearby hilltop.

43. A Little Bit Of Russia In Wuhan

The Alexander Nevsky Russian Orthodox Church on Poyang Street is the oldest Russian Orthodox Church that still exists outside of Russia. It is small but is typically in the style of churches used in Russia. It is a cool piece of Wuhan's history dating from 1876.

To reach the church you should take Metro lines 2 or 6 to Jianghan Road and leave by exit D. you will now be on Jianghan Pedestrian Street, walk in the direction of the river until you reach Poyang Street to your left. Walk along this street for about 10 minutes and the church is on your right. You will pass a Catholic Church also on the same street. There have been no services held here since the early 1950's due to the then political situation in China. It has recently been renovated by the city government, so maybe in the future it will be more than just a tourist attraction.

44. Time To Barter

Hankou's Yasunari Road Night Market is open daily from 5pm until 11pm. It is close to Jianghan Road Metro station on lines 2 and 6. It is in an area of lower to middle priced stores and if you are here in the evening it is a great experience to haggle, if you barter well you may get a 50% reduction off the original quoted price. There are great bargains to be had here, just remember what you are bartering for will not be genuine, everything you see is good quality but fake.

45. Uprising Gate

The area around the Uprising Gate which is next to the Uprising Memorial Hall is a nice area for walking; it is not too busy and very clean and tidy. It is called QiYiMen in Chinese and is about 500 metres from the ShouYiLu metro station which is one stop away from Wuchang Railway station on line 4. It is a free attraction with some old style buildings close by. It was opened in 2011, on the 100th anniversary of the revolution. There is a wooden walkway around a pagoda with plaques showing historic scenes in the city's historic past. This leads up to the memorial itself, made of granite with a map showing the area as it was in 1911. At the end of the memorial garden is a large white pagoda and monuments of natural stone.

46. The Home Of A Former Leader

The vacation residence of Mao Zedong (Chairman Mao) close to the east Lake Hotel on Donghu Road in Wuhan is worth a visit just for the scenery. You can see photos of China's former leader while he was in a relaxed atmosphere and away from the political world of his daily life. The meiling (mayflower) trees help fill the air with a sweet fragrance and there are some beautiful views over the lake. If you visit at the right time of year you can also witness the sight of lotus flowers in full bloom.

It is not the easiest place to find, you have to walk behind the Hubei Provincial Museum and then behind the East Lake Hotel. The site was named Meiling after the trees that decorate the garden. On the winding drive up to the residence you can view some of his calligraphy and you can also see some of the pine trees he planted. His touring car is on show in a large glass building and when open you can view some areas inside the house. It is a calm location away from the noise of a busy city.

47. Dazhimen Railway Station

This used to be the main entrance to Hankou Railway Station but the station was moved instead of enlarging and renovating this one. The impressive old building on Jinghan Street in Jiang'an district of Hankou is full of interesting architecture surrounded by buildings that are very unimpressive. So it stands out immediately. It is a wonderful example of the history of Wuhan.

48. An Unusual Historic Site

The unusually named Peasant Movement Training Institute Site on Hong Lane in Wuchang is open daily from 8am until 6pm. You can just walk and view the site at any time during the opening hours; you may witness a school group sitting in the lecture hall on the hard benches and imagine how it must have felt for the Chinese peasant's sitting there in their grey uniforms getting lectured here for real under the watchful eyes of Mao's statue. There is a dormitory where you can see the harsh living conditions, a dining hall and offices. Outside is a parade ground where the peasants would have learned how to march.

49. Learn Some Science and Technology

Wuhan Museum of Science and Technology is located at Zhaojiatiao in Jiang'an District, it is free but you do need to bring some ID to enter the museum. It is a very good place to visit if you have kids, they will love interacting with the exhibits that allow this. It is set over three floors with two sections of exhibits on each floor. It closes at 4.30pm so to fully enjoy your time here you should arrive before 2pm; there is sometimes a queue to get tickets to enter.

50. Donghu National Park

Donghu National Park in the suburbs to the East of Wuchang district and is located next to the East Lake. It has lots of green areas and a bicycle/walking path. It is another place to relax away from the busy life of the city. It is a beautiful place to visit at any time of the year although my advice would be to bring a bicycle as there is a lot of cycle or walking paths to negotiate. Try to include the sunset in your visit it truly is a beautiful sight to witness across the lake. You can easily discover the time of the sunset from your hotel but as a guide during the summer it is no later than 7.30pm and about 2 hours earlier in the winter. Attractions include an aerial tramway, a musical show in the Chulian temple and a play area for small children. Most of these are open all year but off season they may only be operating at weekends or on holidays, the park however is open every day, it can be very busy at weekends.

SMITHER

TOP REASONS TO BOOK THIS TRIP

Shopping:

There are so many great shopping experiences that you can have in the city of Wuhan, these are particularly so in the city centers of both Wuchang and Hankou. You have a wonderful selection of modern malls full of designer label outlets to tiny stalls selling street food; it really is something for everyone. The transportation available to get to these locations is also very good with the choice of a modern clean metro or the numerous local bus services.

Parks and Open Spaces:

Wuhan has several parks and open spaces to enable you to relax and escape the busy hectic life of the modern city. Where you can simply walk and enjoy the views across one of the many lakes or you can be more energetic and take part in some of the many activities that are available at these locations.

Culture Through Wuhan's Museums and Historical Buildings:

There are 47 museums and numerous historical buildings in Wuhan, so there is truly something for all tastes and interests, whatever your age. The exhibits are from historical artifacts or informing visitors of the city's past to art museums, former residences to interesting oddities like the tax museum. Some of the city's historical attractions require several hours for a visit while others are much smaller and can be viewed in just a few minutes. Many of these are free to enter and just require you to carry your ID or passport to visit.

> TOURIST
GREATER THAN A TOURIST

Visit GreaterThanATourist.com:

http://GreaterThanATourist.com

Sign up for the Greater Than a Tourist Newsletter:

http://eepurl.com/cxspyf

Follow us on Facebook:

https://www.facebook.com/GreaterThanATourist

Follow us on Pinterest:

http://pinterest.com/GreaterThanATourist

Follow us on Instagram:

http://Instagram.com/GreaterThanATourist

SMITHER

> TOURIST
GREATER THAN A TOURIST

Please leave your honest review of this book on Amazon and Goodreads. Thank you. We appreciate your positive and constructive feedback. Thank you.

NOTES

Made in the USA
Las Vegas, NV
20 December 2021